ISBN-13: 979-8-9915846-0-9 (Paperback)

Cover design by: Europeana
Printed in the United States of America

I0151306

CONTENTS

FEAR. TRUST. ANXIETY. LOVE. THE GREATEST OF THESE IS LOVE

◆ ◆ ◆

GRATEFUL POET

FEAR.

Fear you have no place here
Your kingdom has ruled this domain
I'm afraid the end of your reign is near
For there is a kingdom; He has a greater name

Your darkened wastelands have been overtaken
The bright pastures have vacated your land
One thing is for sure: do not be mistaken
This kingdom built on rocks will topple yours in sand

You thrive on the devastation of your people
His kingdom transforms them into love
You may have thought we were like sheeple
But in His kingdom, we are a beautiful dove

A heart that's broken by your betrayal
It will only be mended stronger by the One I mention
Because of our faults, He took a nail
His kingdom finally relieved the tension

So I have left your kingdom for He who is greater
I hope you're paying attention. I need you to read this See, I am
sure you will try to come back later
I bow to one Lord, and His name is Jesus.

IMPERFECT

We all want to be perfect
Setting standards out of reach
Only to be made more and more imperfect

Satan uses this to make us feel worthless
He feeds on it like a filthy leech
Broken souls worthy of a guilty verdict

Jesus set forth a plan that has already surfaced
From a manger to a mount, did he so teach
A Man Ever So Perfect

We drove the nails, created the conflict
On the cross, He hung for the imperfections of each
Broken souls worthy of a guilty verdict

The tomb was sealed shut, and Death it was finished
Our hope of perfection looked so bleak
Forever left Imperfect

Then the unthinkable happened: no one could predict
The stone rolled away, and our sins were bleached
A broken soul worthy of a guilty verdict
Only to remain Perfectly Imperfect

FATHER FORGIVE ME

Father, forgive me, for I know what I am doing.
For I know You feed the birds,
and yet I worry about the food I will eat.
I know worrying will not add another second,
but my anxiety is a ticking clock.
I know I should love my neighbor as myself,
but my isolation from the world takes its toll.
I know I should talk to You,
but I worry my words will not be enough.
I know that it is Christ that gives me strength,
but I rely on my willpower.
Father forgive me
For I do not know Your ways,
but I know they are greater than mine.
I do not fully understand the depth of Your love,
but I am grateful.
I do not know Your plans for me,
but I am hopeful.
I do not know why You picked me,
but I am ready.
I do not know who I am,
and yet I am Yours.
Father, forgive me, but when it comes to Your way,
I know not what I'm doing,
but I will trust You do

DEAD OF NIGHT

I lose myself to the dead of the night
Darkness grows as realization sets in
Another day overrun with fright
My ways are destructive in the dead of night

The day went great. I had some laughs
But I didn't pray again. I must have forgotten
My happiness was always sacrificed like a little calf's
The night grows darker as satan laughs

In the end, we all have a struggle
One that can undermine the depths of a soul
We are not meant to have this much to juggle
This could be the night He ends the Struggle

The morning will come, so please fear not
Close your eyes and try again tomorrow
When you open them, you will be less troubled
For in the night, leave you, I did not

Pray through the night if that is what it takes
Cease the enemy before it is too late
Sometimes for the bondage breaks
The bad nights are what it takes

ANXIETY.

I give you now your daily bread
Do not fret on the road ahead
This kingdom is built on trust
Like a fine metal, you will not rust

The fear will drive you completely mad
The battle over anxiety was already had
Do not be anxious about a thing
Look at the birds. Do they not eat and sing?

I see your mind. I know it scrambles
Tales, heads, tales, it's left you in shambles
My kingdom calls for you to join
Leave the anxiety, forget the coin

Choose the Head that brought you life
Tales has left you in a strife
The battle rages, and we need your joy
I am attacking fear join the convoy

Join the army and take your place
My kingdom's greater join my pace
Trust in Me, and you will find
No sheep is left behind, not you or the Ninety-Nine

REMEMBRANCE PATH

Remember your promises, oh Lord
They are the path that guides me
The map to my destiny

Remember my heart, oh God
It is the thorns that block the way
Yet, filled with roses ready to bloom

Remember your words, oh Lord
The very bricks that lead my feet
Every step is firm and true

Remember my tears, oh God
They flood the road when I've lost my way
Yet, they strengthen this long journey

Remember your love, oh Lord
It is the lamp carried along the path
The light that leads me to You

Remember me, Oh God
My own error disrupts Your perfect path
Yet, Your grace always brings me back

TO BE A FATHER
LIKE YOU

Oh, how I long to be a father like You
One that will not hesitate to protect his young
A father who's rich and loving and slow to anger
Oh, how I wish I were You
Anxiety constantly clouds a father's judgment
Did I spend enough time with them?
Was I too hard on them?
Was I not firm enough?
Oh, how I long to be a father like You
Filled with grace and love, they say You are
A father who lovingly does not conform
to every wish that could harm the child
Oh, how I wish I could love like that
God, I do not want to blink and miss them grow
As time withers, can I better prepare them?
Can I learn Your way and teach them at the same time?
Or has the timer run too far over?
Oh, how long to be a father like You
For I may never understand why You do things
But in my heart, I know there was a reason
For Your love shines bright
And Your convictions are a jagged sword
Oh how I long to be a father like You.

FAITHFULNESS.

It's the oldest story, one as old as dirt
With a bite of an apple, a man tried to find his worth
He came from dust and to it shall return
A moment of glory for a world full of hurt

The springs became pools of blood.
And the flowers they grew thorns
We made our choice and disobeyed
So from the heavens came the rain and the flood

Indeed, many thought it was the end
But Your faithfulness persisted again and again
It sprung from the ground and soared through the sky
As numerous as the stars, we began to mend

The basics of the law were given in faith
In hopes we could grow in You
The law began to replace the love You were growing
We put You on trial as if there were even a case

Then along came a king and a Son of royalty
Through him, the story starts to make sense
The covenants grew, and Your faithfulness too
How can we match Your loyalty

The Promise was here and died
To rise and proclaim that death is defeated
Our mistakes were numbered, and You did not give up You loved
us in the womb just as a kid

So how could I repay a debt such as this
Other than following the Spirit that handles these fruits I can
learn from these gifts and maybe give it back
Oh, Your faithfulness; it is heaven's kiss

MAJESTIC (PSALM 8)

Oh Lord, how majestic is Your name
Mountains move just for You
You heal the broken and the lame

It is You above fortune and fame
They will praise You singing,
Oh Lord, how majestic is Your name

We may sin, but You love us all the same
For Your son came to earth and,
You healed the broken and the lame

Father, the heavens celebrate Your victories
For the angels sing of Your goodness
Oh Lord, how majestic is Your name

The oceans obey Your command
That's why we're baptized in water, so,
You heal the broken and the lame

The worldly things are all I can explain
To describe Your mercy that freed us from shame
Oh Lord, Our Lord, how majestic is Your name
For it is You that heals the broken and the lame

OUTNUMBERED

Outnumbered
Oh, how they conspire
The enemies multiply by the day
Taunting endlessly
Surrounded
Oh, how they taunt
Their chariots rush toward me
Besieged
Oh, how they laugh
Chants fill the skies with threats
Failure
They scream around me
It seems like all hope is lost,

but then,

Defeated
The enemy was not around
For I was surrounded by three in one body
Redemption
A glorious Savior sent
To save this lost soul from man's enemy
Holy
I cry out, You have won
The soldiers have no place in this mind
For the thoughts of Your grace leave me
Outnumbered

RAINBOW BABY

Rainbows, they come after the flood

And losing you left us lost at sea

Imagine losing a part of your family

Nothing can change what happened

But the rainbow must come

One day, we will meet our babies

We think you'd love the rainbows that came

Believe that we wish you were here too

All these babies sure could use the snuggles

Bad things happen; I'm glad that you're safe

You were the storm. I hope you love your rainbow.

WANDERING ALBATROSS

In my heart, I cannot explain
The ways Your love has changed me
I may still mess up
Your grace, though, covered the fee

Your power is unfathomable
God's creation I will never fully comprehend
Full of wonder and color
Your grace, it has no end

A love beyond my reach, a love I can never match
Laid out on an old, rugged cross
My soul is made new
For the old, I count it all a loss
Your grace, beautiful as a wandering albatross

PATIENCE.

Waiting has never been a skill of mine
Why have tomorrow when today is here
Stuck in traffic; who's got the time
Sometimes, I cannot bear it when the time is near

I live by the calendar, awaiting another day
Maybe it will be better; I cannot wait
My food is taking so long. What can I say?
Do it right, but do not be late.

This is a weakness that is for sure
Soon for You, my King is a lifetime for me I know
Your Spirit is my only cure
To cure impatience, for clarity to see

I pray I have more time to learn
I'll take my time and work on it today
Patience is a fruit that I want; I yearn
Time is money, and this is the price I pay

My kids helped me grow this fruit even further
They require patience, and I owe it to them
Can You help me perfect this with great fervor
I'll start with amen, for by this, Your fruit stem

THE CUP

Father, take this cup from me
The wine is too dry
The bottom of the glass is all I see

Father, take away the burden
The glass used to be half-full
Now, it seems to be where I place my hurt in

Father, the cup is getting heavy
The wine only gets me drunk
Everything seems so unsteady

Father, give me some bread
Let it soak up the alcohol
Hurry so I can get out of my head

Father, this is not my cup to carry
For you already laid it down
I'll walk the drunken road, but know that it is scary

FROM THE WARDROBE TO THE SHIRE.

From the Wardrobe to the Shire
I traveled through the dark forest
The ring it seemed to call my name.
How could I resist a temptation so great?
The eye calls me closer to Mordor

Those Turkish delights they taste so great
I ate, and I ate that never-ending supply
It seemed so great
Until that wretched witch took them away

So what do these injustices call for
We could ask Tolkien or Lewis
If they were here today
But I do think the answers are in the books

That evil is squandered within these pages
A tortured soul burned with the ring
The stone table split for the rest of Narnia
The lands were renewed with a great revival

The stories tell of countless victories of Aslan
Oh, how he sang over creation
Or the wisdom of Gandalf
His words of courage spared my life

Even the smallest can change our hearts
Why even Lucy rode an untamed lion into battle
The spiritually damned even win our hearts
I can't help but love my poor, precious
Cause even a traitor can mend

These Works of fiction taught me goodness
Quotes in my mind that will last a lifetime
I am thankful for these stories of old
As Your Voice echoes through the authors

From the Wardrobe to the Shire
I explored the realms of imagination
I looked for You in every chapter
And I saw You at every turn of the way

BRICK BY BRICK
(2 SAMUEL 7)

Brick by brick
I carry them one at a time
Oh the burdens of building
The weight of the stone crushing my back

Brick by brick
I carry with a tune on my lips
For this building is all for You
The sweat on my brow is but a minor issue

Brick by brick
I build the temple
One man was not meant for this job alone
Why oh Lord is it so difficult?

Brick by brick
You grab them one at a time
The burden was not mine to carry
Was it not I you intended this for?

Brick by brick
The the temple fell down
Because it was not mine to build
It belonged to the future generations

Brick by brick
I was to lay the foundation
For those who will build the house
Only then will the family last a lifetime

Brick by brick
I will build my family in Your name always So that others may see
the work of Your love
The temple it was never mine to build

I wasn't meant to carry these burdens
So, I will lay them at Your Feet
Brick by brick

MUSTARD SEED

How can I plant the mustard seeds?
You say I need to for Your kingdom to grow
But how when my land is covered in weeds

I want to see lots of branches
One day the seeds I will sow
I have already passed many chances

The birds need their shade
So, to the field, I will go
To find seeds planted on a rocky grade

With this bit of faith, I have much to prove
This spring, I will dig out the hoe
Only then will the mountains move

The replanting must be done
See, my seeds are not yet in a row
But the planting has already begun.

TRUST.

What a King I now serve
I have given up that forsaken place
Sometimes, I return, but only for a moment
Trust is complex, with a steep learning curve

A king deserves so much treasure
Yet what do I have to give?
I can give my all, but it does not add up
Trust is hard, almost impossible to measure

Truth be told, I should not worry
The kingdom I came from was not so great
You were triumphant and saved me
Trust is hard, but what's the hurry?

I'll praise You, for you have my best interest
A beautiful family you have given me
I hope you will take care of them too
Trust is hard, but your kingdom has a witness

I will give my all to have trust in You
On whatever mission the kingdom needs
My heart will honor You until it returns
Trust is hard, but it's the least I can do

LIGHTS ORIGIN

Where God does the light come from?
Is it the absence of the dark?
Is it the sunlight to which darkness must succumb
Shine bright and give me light

When does the light prevail?
Must we wait for another generation?
Darkness won again, just another drop in the pale
Shine bright and give me light

Is there a number to which You assigned the stars?
Was there not enough to cover the darkness completely?
From the ends of space to the surface of Mars,
Shine bright and give me light

Where God does the light come from?
It comes from You, even in the dark
Even if right now it is only some,
When the time comes, and this dark fades,
May You shine bright, and Your glory come

INTEND

Why do I do the things I do not intend?
And not do the things to get to the goals end
Father, at your feet my burdens I send
For I am a wretched man deserving the end
I call on to you help me do the things I intend

JOY.

Midnight strikes, and the thief draws near
I am safe, though I locked the door
In the safe, my joy awaits the next day
At least until the thief gets here

It is a quiet night; I'm safe and happy
My whole world is a peaceful bliss
In the King's name, I do rejoice
I was saved from hell; my last king was snappy

Doors creak, and the traps have been set
With a bag, he comes to take my joy
On his way to the safe, he goes
He's in for a treat; he will regret

My joy is untouchable regardless of his ploys
He comes to me upset and unhinged
"Boy, where is your joy? I have come to take it."
I should be afraid, but his words are just noise

"I fear you no more; I see past your disguise."
See, my joy is in Him who creates joy
And the man standing before me is no threat
For he was gone the moment I closed my eyes

FLOWERING DOGWOOD

It is the coming of spring
The cold is gone; it will be back soon
Yellow dandelions begin to grow
Do not focus on that hard winter
I know it was rough
But the sunflowers are yet to come
For the plants and trees were dead
Violets swarm in patches
The snow was pretty until it never left
Death is defeated, yet another spring
For growth and life have taken control
It will not last; it is just a season
But for now
I'll admire this flowering dogwood
That so eloquently resides in my yard

CARRY ME

Would you carry me?
Carry me along your blessed path
The path I cannot walk alone
In my spirit, I trust you
To guide me in every way
Although my heart may fail
You are my shield
You carry my out-of-battle
Be my Shepard
Carry me towards your will
Lead me to green pastures vast and still,
Where worries fade like whispers on the breeze
And in Your embrace,
I find my refuge,
Your Spirit
my peace,
Your sacrifice
My salvation.
If I let go, would you carry me?

GRATITUDE (ODE)

It is you I must ***Thank***
I would not be where I am if not for ***You***
For grace has made me new
All the ***loving*** I have grown to know
I have not always been the best ***me at*** times
Even at ***my lowest***, you were present
Your love ***For*** the world is the map
It is what is ***guiding me*** to free others
At all costs, I will follow your will
With ***my*** last breath, I will sing,
With my hands lifted at the ***Highest***
That Brandon Lake song ***I*** love so much
My praise ***could never*** be enough
I still must ***Express*** to You
That ***all of*** the things you've done for me
My gratitude will be forever yours

FORGIVE MY HEART (HAIKU)

Jesus forgive me
My heart is not as it should
Make it like Your own

SELF-CONTROL.

Of all the fruits, this one is so sour
Where one is a minute, this is an hour
Just add sugar. It takes away the sour face
But the Spirit will just put you back in place

It's not that it's terrible it really is pleasant
The fruit of control is still present
When I make it my own, the danger arises
My life becomes full of compromises

One thing that should still hold is the law
The spirit convicts me to grow this flaw
The fruit that is sour for you
It mustn't be sweetened. It must be cared for, too

This cherry and lemon that Spirit laid out
It must be digested, no doubt
So practice self-control in all that's to come
The sour is good; the sweet cannot become

In this case, sour is good if it holds the truth
Anger and anxiety may want to sleuth
And take hold of your life; do not give it away
I give You control of this fruit, okay
May You be the potter and I the clay

THE PERFECT STORM

Rain
Drip, Drip, Drip
The thoughts pour like a spring rain
These words get stuck in my brain
The storm begins

Hail
Crack, Crack, Crack
Constant reminders of the hits I've taken
All the lies build up; am I mistaken?
The storm builds

Lighting
Flash, Flash, Flash
Memories flicker of the good and bad
Clouds roll in, and I start to get mad
The storm rages

Thunder
Clap, Clap, Clap
A reminder that I am small compared to nature
Make it end or my soul, I will wager
The storm rages on

But then...

Rainbow
Red, Orange, Violet
Colors cover the sky so vivid
My family is a reminder to stay committed The storm dissipates

Sunshine
Shine, Shine, Shine
My God has blessed me beyond belief
The storm did not win; it was merely a lousy thief
The storm perfect

Without it, the rainbow wouldn't be so vivid,
and the sunshine would be dim.

IDOLS

We all have them: a golden calf
Pulling us from the Lord
Whispering sweet promises, all too deft.
Even just one hit of this cigarette, even if just half

Distractions spun in the golden cord.
Wrapping our minds in hopeless illusion
Dopamine surges with these pictures
We live by Facebook and die by the sword

Fix the masks we wear with steadfast disillusion
Convinced we do not need God to get out
The devil's greatest lie was idols had to be big
A person and heroin combined in a state of fusion

Metal and silver, it all seems too easy
With the tap of a card, I can have everything
Chasing the dollars to a penniless end
The card is my master looking to cease me

Sex, drugs, and alcohol that's the good life
That's how Hollywood portrays it anyway
The devil has a hold on every generation
Actors and actresses don't care about the strife

We all have them, this burden to bear
A crutch to get us through, an addiction
Whatever affliction has caused you much grief
I have mine too and I will keep you in prayer;
A man like me could cast no judgment

Go to the altar and leave the calf for God to deal
It cannot run you; you're a slave no longer
You've been starving; the Lord will feed you
So devil beware, for your grip has been loosened
For it is by Jesus' name that we heal.

THE MIDDLE

The middle can leave you sweaty but cold
It is like a spring day dew and frost in the morning
By noon, the sun is blazing
In the middle, dehydration strikes,
and thirst is quenched
It is like being in a desert, thirsty and alone
This desert may have flowing rivers,
but you only sometimes take a drink
In the middle, there is highs and lows
The center of the mountain is higher than the start
But the peak is still a long climb
In the middle, you are tired and awake
Everything is dark and hazy
But some things bring a gloriously sobering reality
In the middle, you may wander and already be home
Lost in your own house, trying to find the door
While cozying in on the new leather couch
In the middle life lasts the longest
The highs and lows are only temporary
Something has to connect the two
Sometimes, we must enjoy this center path
Or we may miss life's greatest treasures
After all,
The middle is where life truly begins

GENTLENESS.

I grab my washboard and here I go
Another daily task to bog me down
I cannot think of a task more low
But I will do my laundry with a frown

My clothes need to be cleaned that's the facts
I would like some help if You can
For the piles getting bigger beside the empty racks
Had it not been for You, I'd have already ran

I started to look at this task as something new
Yeah, the pungent smells do grow old
With the right outlook, it may be what I want to do
This daily task You may have me sold

I'm taking what's filthy and making it clean
They go from what they are to nice and soft
The gentleness is a beauty I've never seen
Your word is in the washboard from aloft

The soap cleans just as Jesus did
While the softener brings a gentle Spirit
My gentleness, the world did try to rid
All the while, this fruit makes us coherent

THE TOWER

'Twas the tower that I came across
That beautiful blonde hair caught my eye
Out the window, it went with a toss

Her beauty was unmatched
The intimidation made me hesitate
Fear of possibly getting attached

I started to run, but God had other plans
"Her heart is unlike any other."
"Love her and her other two lambs."

My heart broken, I cried let down your hair
When she did, I climbed that tower
Into her eyes did I lovingly stare

"My lady, you are everything I see."
"I may have run, but one thing is sure."
"I wish that forever you will be with me."

"Why did you return and give me my ring?"
She seemed so uncertain about why she was saved
"God assured me you're the queen to this king."

We married, had four lambs, as our life went on
She was mistaken on the story of this fairy tale
"For you, Savannah, that saved me that dawn."

GOODNESS.

We all want our stake in gold
To build a legacy and a wealth so grand
Some thoughts are good, and others evil
Stuck in a poker match, we constantly fold

Copper and silver just do not cut it
They are worthless in the grand scheme
It may not be true but that's how it seems
If money is all this life is, then maybe we quit

Truth be told, I hear there is more
A bank with a Banker, a heart of gold
The pennies will be first, and the dollars last
Every other pound would seem a bore

Open an account and have a seat
The bank is open and He wants to share
The gold is goodness, and its fruit is pure
You know the story, a Samaritan in the street?

This is how it indeed should be
A Banker and His people with this golden ache,
Give more and receive less, and indeed I will see
That goodness and mercy shall follow me

MY FATHER'S HOUSE

Welcome to my Father's house
He is loving and a great host
He has wine and bread
Yes, welcome
Have a seat, take a load off
I apologize the house is a mess
My father does the cleaning
I have not let him, as you can see
He prefers this house as pure as a lamb
I've just been so busy
I'll let him try another day
Have you seen the snake?
He is a pet I chose to take in
Father told me no, but what is the harm?
It's time to eat. We should grab a plate

Oh, you want to pray?
I have not done that since adopting the snake
See, he requires so much
I must feed him, or he will get angry
I'll have to get rid of him when
I find my father
Where is he, you say?
Oh, he's not been in a while
He despises snakes and goes away
I know you came to see my Father
And I'm sorry, but here is the truth
My Father's house is empty
For it is not a place
My Father resides in my heart
Or at least he used to before the snake

OH GOD, MY GOD
(PSALM 51)

Oh God, my God
Have I not learned a thing
My transgressions add up by the day
Is there not an end to death's sting?
Or is it my burdens in which I must lay?

Oh God, my God
Please do not hide Your face
I believe my heart is still searching
I'm looking to finish the race
But I can feel the enemy lurching

Oh God, my God
Will You give me a clean heart
I hope You can accept my repentance
I'm hoping for a fresh start
A means to an end of this life sentence

Oh God, my God
Make me clean as the snow
I look forward to Your delight
And Father, I want You to know
This broken heart is contrite

Oh God, my God
I may have failed You
My strength may have wavered
Indeed, I will pay my due
But, thank God, I'm still favored

SUN AND MOON

If the moon and sun obey, shouldn't I?
My heart just takes the steering wheel
Does anger sink deeper as the day passes by?

I don't know how to act when I start to feel
If the stars were made to worship, why can't I?
As life grabs a hold, my layers start to peel

Can I fight emotion and break from this lie?
It clouds my judgment to know if you are real
Lord, I know the answers, so help me try

When the day gets bad, will you take the wheel?
Can I say a prayer so it's you I feel?
Will I feel the lousy judgment start to peel?
Once I change my questions, I know You are real.
And I will leave my fate to You until the day I die.

HOPE.

Here, here, make way
The king is here, but He is not as you'd expect
He brings me fruits and fights for me
The servant Lord, my hope, every day

It's the waving of palms and early morn'
When the Lord rides in on a meek colt
He brings promises of a better life
An Earth that is truly a sight to adorn

The past is gone. It left a beautiful presence
It changed me in ways I cannot explain
The present and the future are the same
My hope is driven by His Holy Essence

A reason to smile and hope for the best
You will not find it in any other
For little doses come from many others
But the holy kind of hope will give you rest

Here here, come join in
The fruits await. I am hopeful for the next
It comes at a cost small and large
A worthy price for this hope from Him

MOMENTS

I'd love to go back to those moments
Sunday mornings with Golden Girls going
Those days, the morning coffee was filled with love
Big breakfasts and smiles straight out of bed
You and the girls are the most significant components

The older kids were growing more self-sufficient
Giving us nights to find our rhythm
You were something of a beauty
With that fireplace glowing off your skin
Our relationship grew to be very efficient

I could not help but to get down on my knee
Amongst the flowers and the lights
Our wedding came near in that very spot
Little did we know that day,
Just how hectic our life could be

Two more babies entered our home.
Slowly, our date nights began to fade
Our focus switched to them and how amazing they are
The four queens took over this realm
You and I were never alone

It's a season in our life where we take care of kids
We have survived and missed some moments
But that's okay because we still find time
Our story of marriage is oh-so-sweet
Because it still only truly begins

I adore the wife and mother you are
Life's not always easy, but you make it so
Cause for me, every day, the decision is made
Every season made so much richer
My Christmas' more bright because you are the star

So whatever enemy or whatever opponents
I can't wait to face them by your side
For now, let's enjoy this chaotic season
For, one day, we will look back and say
I'd love to go back to those moments

THE ELEMENTS

The elements
Legend says only one could master them
There may be four, and here's why
I've seen the avatars, and they are girls
They conquer the elements, both good and bad

Fire
I see passion roaring within your eyes
A future so bright and burning inside
You are my world, and I hope you know that
Oh, but there's more elements I must add

Air
On your air scooter, do you laugh and play
Air is the joy I see in you
May it keep you afloat way in the sky
It's a force of nature for which I am glad

Water
It is the tears I wipe from your eyes
Bending may fail you; you mustn't run
You will fall, get up, and put the fire out
You have all four elements when you are sad

Earth
I see your strength in every rock
You are warriors. I know it's true
So put on your makeup and go to battle
I know it's in there; I've seen you mad

I know you do all of these things
But you are my girls, and I want you to know
I love you all, and I will always worry
You may be the avatars, but I'm still your dad

PEACE.

"Oh, how you cower at the sound of my voice."
The enemy whispered to me
"You'll never find peace; you'll never be free."
I almost believed him, but I had a choice

"Where will you go, boy? You're too wicked."
Constantly, he tried to tear me down
"You will never escape my sound."
Chaotic and loud, I wished I was acquitted

So I went to that river to find the answer
"Get away from that water! What are you doing!"
I found a Peace that is worth pursuing
And I dove into that water to cure the cancer

The water roars against my soul
It was a glorious rush to feel that release
For by that river, I finally felt peace
As I rose from the water, I claimed what he stole

The light was bright, and I heard a voice
"My peace I give to you; may you find rest."
By his Spirit was I truly blessed
And in the Lord's name will I rejoice

TROUBLED BONES
(PSALM 6)

O Lord, heal me with Your love
For I have troubled bones
Send Your spirit upon me like a dove
For I am weary from these moans

O Lord, wipe these teary eyes
For I have a troubled soul
Turn me from my foe's lies
For I need what the enemy stole

O Lord, be Gracious to me
For I cannot praise You from the grave
You cleaned my eyes, and now I see
So I'll pray to the Lord, my soul, to save

PRAISE (HAIKU)

How can I thank You
God You have blessed me greatly
I will give You praise

KINDNESS.

A single honeycomb is all a bee needs
Preserving the food for a rainy day
It gives life when the world brings weeds
It is sweet to the soul and keeps them going

Nature's nectar, just a drop will do
Keeping bees warm when the world is so cold
I wonder what that could do for you?
Have a taste, and we can see how it goes

It is quite delectable on some cornbread,
In a splash of tea, maybe with a friend
Or perhaps a gift to some on their deathbed
So many ways to use this ingredient

Bees swarm and can be deadly
But oh, how sometimes they create a treat
Some say honey is a fruit medley
It gives people joy and can bring hope

Honey is pleasant, just like kindness
When the world is salty, we need some sweet
This may be the way to cure our blindness
If we could all learn this, wouldn't it be neat?

SPARROW
(PSALM 102)

The world looks so big from way up here
Perched on this roof, I see it all
I hear the taunting you do to me
All the while, you're full of cheer

I do not do a thing but fly
Yet they fire shots at me quite frequently
I'm just a bird living my life
I want to eat bread and soar in the sky

I wonder what it feels like to have arms
To reach out in love to those around you
I thought you must hug everyone you see
Yet I've seen nothing but hate from cities to farms

What does a bird like me have to do?
To take the place of such ignorant beings
You have the capability of so much more
Me, a mere sparrow, could do it better than you

All the while, I should be grateful as I go to bed
I may not be a human-like Adam or Eve
But the Lord provides, and He gave me flight
He's even got the hairs numbered on your head

Look, another sparrow came to join me
I am not alone; I have a companion
It seems just a bit of gratitude may go far
From the east to the west and from sea to sea

I may be just a lonely little sparrow
But we share this earth with the same creator
Praise Him, for I don't think He messed up
Humans are friends, and I will not be jealous
I will fly above you as you walk through the sea
Only to make sure you're safe from the Pharaoh

I WISH I WERE...

Oh, how I wish I were a psalmist
To write beautiful poems to guide generations
A beautiful melody of praise or,
A powerful presence before my enemies
If I were David, I could slay my giants
I could sing of your love forever
I would dance before you
My heart would be right after your own heart
Oh, how I wish I had the wisdom of Proverbs
If I had an ounce like Solomon
I could build your temple
I would pray a prayer of dedication to You
My lineage would be the Son of God
Oh, how I wish I were a disciple
If I were, I would be like Peter
I could see for my eyes, my Lord
I would follow you until my punishment
My name would be forever changed

But if I were
A psalmist, I would not have Your spirit
David, I would be a murderer
Solomon, a blatantly disobeying king
Peter, a denier and a sinner
Maybe we are pretty similar
I abandon Your Spirit constantly
But You are a powerful presence anyway
I murder the Spirit with my pride and sin
But, You are still in my heart
I disobey Your Spirit
But, You bring me to Your family table
I deny and sin against the Spirit
But,
You changed my name forever.

GOD'S HEART

The heavens shook as God's heart was shattered
The world fell into turmoil
Broken and tattered

The day you left, I will never forget
The words of your death
Indeed, our Maker, you have finally met

I'm sure He rejoiced
You were finally home
I hope the songs were beautifully voiced

But even though you were home,
God's heart broke, and mine, too
For you should have never felt that alone

FRUITS.

A blank void filled with countless thoughts
you may be wondering how this is possible
Take a step into a poet's mind, and you will see
A dark pit full of ideas and sometimes empty
Writer's block is a hell of a thing
Grab the pen and start writing

Patience...
Crinkle.
In the trash, it goes
What could I write next?
Perhaps happiness is brewing, Joy..
Crinkle.
Off to the next
I can not write about that today
Let's move on to the next, Kindness..
Crinkle.
I'll write that some other time
Perhaps a focus on something greater
I could write about that, hmm or... Self-control..
Crinkle.
No, that one's not as fun
Maybe a great poem is what I need
How about one about such a thing, Goodness..
Crinkle.
There was nothing good about today
Writing is difficult without proper guidance
Would You be able to teach me about this in the next one?
Peace..
Crinkle.
I could use it, but I'm so chaotic
I have an idea I think I finally got it

A poem should be soft and speak to the heart,
Gentleness..
Crinkle.
The pencil is too sharp, and anything but
It seems my writing may be dependent on me
But You still insist on helping because of Your
Faithfulness..
Crinkle.
I am not worthy
This writing was furious and crazy hard

The fruits seemed so simple
I was missing the poem, the most important of all
The one that all the fruits stem
It took years for me to finally see
That the poem I needed was still trapped inside
I needed a teacher, a savior, a Spirit
I gave the pen over to him, and off we went

The poems they filled the pages
The pen I could not put down
The titles came back
For Faithfulness.
I am grateful
By Gentleness.
I am softer
In Peace.
I am healed
Thank Goodness.
I am saved
By
Self-control.
I am listening
From Kindness.
I am a new man
Among Patience.

I am discerning
With
Joy.
I am alive
Because of these fruits, I was given a chance
To become someone I always wanted to be
A writer who knew some truth from above
To share a message, one of the perfect words
I did not mention the fruit that bears the most
It gives life to all of these fruit
You will find it in the Spirit I mentioned
These fruits are good, but wait and see

That the greatest of these is…

LOVE.

What is it?
A question it seems we all have asked
Easy and challenging, but the greatest of all
The fruits all come back to this

So what could it be?
I could say what it means to me.
When I think of love, much comes to mind
To start, the beauty of the Savannah plains

I love Your creation and the beauty it yields
Like the happiness within the Violet fields
I know there's no mistaking this is from You
No words could ever amount to how great it is

Love is hope, and kind, and full of Grace
I cannot describe it, but let me make my case
My patience grows greater because of Your love
It fills my heart more and more each day

Love is Christmas, a beautiful and joyous Noel
Colorful lights and celebration fill my soul
You have been born and given me life
Destroying the fear that decayed inside

I think of the Garden of Eden and your vision
It is a sight worth seeing, created with such precision
I cannot believe we have such a Creator
But there is more that I should mention

Love is easy when it comes to these things
For my family brings a love I will forever sing
Your goodness precedes even this love
Sometimes, I forget to love for another mile

The ones who spit and give me hate
Even with Judas, Jesus sat and ate
I must give way and be gentle with the enemy
So I can better understand a love so grand

For the greatest of this love is not yet explained
You died and rose, and only one thing remained
A love so great that by you could be obtained
So I will love the broken and the chained

I will love the rich and poor
Give to those who are sick and need more
I will do your will as more than a chore
What else could love be for?